European Cuisine

Authentic European Recipes in an Easy European Cookbook

By
BookSumo Press

Published by
http://www.booksumo.com

ENJOY THE RECIPES?

KEEP ON COOKING
WITH 6 MORE FREE COOKBOOKS!

Visit our website and simply enter your email address to join the club and receive your 6 cookbooks.

LEGAL NOTES

Table of Contents

Spicy Nuts Cake 25

Easy Wienerschnitzel 26

Eastern European Style Lasagna 27

Stovetop Egg Noodles 28

Lunch in Germany 29

Roasted BBQ Chicken with Sauerkraut 30

Countryside Cabbage 31

Curry Sausage 32

Sour Cream and Onion Pie 33

Apples, Pickled Cabbage, and Sausage 34

German Style Salad Dressing 35

German Rump Roast 36

German Style Soup I 38

Bavarian Chocolate Cheese Truffles 39

Bavarian Veggie Soup 40

Bavarian Coconut Truffles 41

Pink Apple
Borscht

Prep Time: 30 mins
Total Time: 2 hrs

Servings per Recipe: 4

Calories	283.6
Fat	16.6g
Cholesterol	7.2mg
Sodium	417.7mg
Carbohydrates	27.1g
Protein	7.8g

Ingredients

1 lb. beet
kosher salt & ground black pepper
6 sprigs thyme, divided
6 tbsp extra virgin olive oil, divided
1 medium onion, chopped
2 carrots, chopped
2 garlic cloves, chopped
6 C. chicken stock, heated

2 tbsp red wine vinegar
1 tbsp honey
1 granny smith apple, peeled
2 tbsp chopped dill
sour cream

Directions

1. Before you do anything, preheat the oven to 400 F.
2. Grease a baking pan. Line up a baking sheet with a piece of foil. Toss in it the beets with 3 tbsp of olive oil, 3 thyme sprigs, a pinch of salt and pepper.
3. Cook them in the oven for 60 min. Place the beets pan aside until they cool down completely. Peel the beets and finely chop them.
4. Place a large pot over medium heat. Heat in it 3 tbsp of olive oil. Add the onion with carrots, garlic, 3 thyme sprigs.
5. Cook them for 12 min. Stir in the chicken stock and cook them for an extra 22 min. Once the time is up, discard the thyme sprigs.
6. Get a food processor: Place in it the chopped beets with cooked veggies and some of their stock, vinegar and honey, a pinch of salt and pepper.
7. Process them until they become smooth. Serve your soup with some sour cream.
8. Enjoy.

BLUSHING
Chicken Borscht

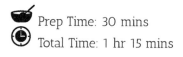

Prep Time: 30 mins
Total Time: 1 hr 15 mins

Servings per Recipe: 6	
Calories	390.7
Fat	6.6g
Cholesterol	25.1mg
Sodium	364.1mg
Carbohydrates	67.3g
Protein	23.0g

Ingredients

2 tbsp extra virgin olive oil
3 garlic cloves, chopped
1 medium onion, chopped
4 packed C. thinly sliced green cabbage
3 medium white potatoes, cubed
2 medium beets, peeled and shredded
1 large carrot, peeled and shredded
1 bay leaf
1 tbsp tomato paste

salt
12 grape tomatoes, halved
2 boneless skinless chicken breast halves, diced
15 oz. great northern beans, rinsed and drained
1/4 C. chopped dill

Directions

1. Place a large pan over medium heat. Heat in it the oil. Cook in it the onion with garlic for 12 min.
2. Stir in the carrots, potatoes, cabbage, and tomato paste. bay leaf and 2 quarts water.
3. Cook them over high heat until they start boiling. Lower the heat and cover the pot partially.
4. Let the soup cook for 16 min. Stir in the chicken, tomatoes and beans and half the dill.
5. Let it cook for 7 to 10 min. Adjust the seasonings of the soup then serve it warm.
6. Enjoy.

Moscow
Beef Kabobs

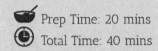 Prep Time: 20 mins

🕐 Total Time: 40 mins

Servings per Recipe: 5

Calories	535.6
Fat	46.7g
Cholesterol	0.0mg
Sodium	478.4mg
Carbohydrates	37.0g
Protein	3.9g

Ingredients

2 lbs. top sirloin steaks, cut into pieces
2 bell peppers, sliced
1 purple onion, large, sliced
15 medium bamboo skewers
Kabobs
1 C. olive oil
1/2 C. lemon juice
1 tsp salt

1 tsp ground black pepper
4 garlic cloves, pressed
3 tbsp dill, chopped
2 dried bay leaves

Directions

1. Get a large mixing bowl: Mix in it all the marinade ingredients.
2. Add to it the beef pieces and toss them to coat. Cover the bowl with a plastic wrap and let it sit for at least an overnight.
3. Once the time is up, place the marinated meat aside to sit for 35 min.
4. Before you do anything, preheat the grill and grease it.
5. Drain the beef pieces from the marinade. Thread them onto skewers with onion and bell pepper.
6. Place the skewers over the grill and cook them for 9 to 12 min while turning them often.
7. Serve your bamboo kabobs with a salad and some bread.
8. Enjoy.

HERBED
Mushroom Salad

Prep Time: 24 hrs
Total Time: 24 hrs

Servings per Recipe: 4
Calories   276.1
Fat   27.5g
Cholesterol   0.0mg
Sodium   446.1mg
Carbohydrates   7.0g
Protein   3.9g

Ingredients

1 lb. mushroom
1/2 C. lemon juice
1/2 C. olive oil
2 green onions, thinly sliced
1/4 C. parsley, chopped
1 medium garlic clove, chopped
3/4 tsp salt

1/4 tsp black pepper
1/4 tsp paprika
2 - 3 bay leaves

Directions

1. Get a mixing bowl: Toss in it the mushroom with lemon juice, olive oil, onion, parsley, bay leaves, salt and pepper.

2. Add the paprika and toss them to coat. Place the salad in the fridge and let it sit for at least 3 h.

3. Serve it with a drizzle of olive oil and some bread.

4. Enjoy.

Pavlova
with Lemon Curd

Prep Time: 30 mins
Total Time: 13 hrs 30 mins

Servings per Recipe: 8
Calories	128.2
Fat	1.9g
Cholesterol	4.9mg
Sodium	54.8mg
Carbohydrates	26.3g
Protein	2.0g

Ingredients

1 C. sugar
1 tbsp cornstarch
4 egg whites, room temperature
1/4 tsp cream of tartar
1 pinch salt
1/4 tsp vanilla extract
parchment paper
1 (10 oz.) jars lemon curd

1/3 C. sour cream
mixed berry
lemon zest

Directions

1. Before you do anything, preheat the oven to 225 F. Grease a baking pan.
2. Get a mixing bowl: Mix in it the sugar with cornstarch.
3. Get a large mixing bowl: Whisk in it the egg whites for 60 sec.
4. Mix in the cream of tartar with salt. Beat them for 30 sec.
5. Add the sugar gradually to the mix while beating them all the time until the egg white peak form. Add the vanilla and mix them.
6. Pour the mixture into the greased pan. Place it in the oven and cook it for 90 min. Turn off the oven and let the cake rest for at least 12 h.
7. Get a mixing bowl: Mix in it the sour cream with lemon curd. Place it in the fridge until the cake is ready.
8. Garnish the pavlova cake with lemon curd and your favorite toppings then serve it.
9. Enjoy.

WARM
Cabbage Salad

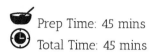
Prep Time: 45 mins
Total Time: 45 mins

Servings per Recipe: 8
Calories	160.3
Fat	7.5g
Cholesterol	19.0mg
Sodium	683.6mg
Carbohydrates	23.1g
Protein	2.1g

Ingredients

5 tbsp butter
2 onions thinly sliced
2/3 C. red wine vinegar
1/2 C. applesauce
2 tbsp sugar
2 tsp salt
1 tsp ground black pepper
1 bay leaf

1/8 tsp ground cloves
2 lbs. about 1 head red cabbage, cut into strips
1 large golden apple, peeled, cored, thinly sliced
1/2 C. apple juice

Directions

1. Place a large pan over medium heat. Heat in it the butter. Cook in it the onion for 12 min
2. add the applesauce with vinegar, sugar, bay leaf, ground cloves, cabbage, salt and pepper. Cook them for 6 min.
3. Put on the lid and let them cook for an extra 18 min.
4. Once the time is up, stir in the apple with apple juice. Cook them for 6 min while stirring it often.
5. Serve your salad warm or cold with some chopped nuts.
6. Enjoy.

Stuffed Eggs

 Prep Time: 20 mins
Total Time: 20 mins

Servings per Recipe: 4
Calories	164.3
Fat	11.5g
Cholesterol	282.7mg
Sodium	516.6mg
Carbohydrates	5.7g
Protein	9.3g

Ingredients

6 hardboiled egg
3 tbsp mayonnaise
1 tbsp dry mustard

3 small pickles, chopped
2 tbsp scallions, chopped

Directions

1. Slice the eggs in half and remove from them the egg yolks.
2. Get a mixing bowl: Mix in it the mayonnaise, egg yolks with pickles, mustard, scallions, a pinch of salt and pepper until they become creamy.
3. Pour the mixture in a piping bag. Fill the egg white halves with it.
4. Garnish them with some chopped scallions then serve them.
5. Enjoy.

GOLDEN
Fiesta Cake

Prep Time: 30 mins
Total Time: 2 hrs 30 mins

Servings per Recipe: 28	
Calories	197.0
Fat	2.9g
Cholesterol	33.7mg
Sodium	65.1mg
Carbohydrates	37.6g
Protein	5.2g

Ingredients

DOUGH
1 C. dried cranberries
1 tbsp Amaretto
1 C. fat-free evaporated milk
1 (8 oz.) cartons low-fat sour cream
2 1/4 tsp dry yeast
1/4 C. warm water
1/2 C. granulated sugar
2 large eggs
2 large egg yolks
1 tsp almond extract

1/2 tsp salt
6 C. all-purpose flour, divided
cooking spray
1 tbsp granulated sugar
1 C. golden raisin
1/2 C. slivered almonds
ICING
1 1/2 C. powdered sugar
1/4 C. fat-free evaporated milk
1/4 tsp almond extract

Directions

1. Before you do anything, preheat the oven to 350 F. Grease a Bundt baking pan, and sprinkle in it 1 tbsp of sugar.
2. To make the dough:
3. Get a small mixing bowl: Stir in it the cranberries with amaretto. Place it aside to soak.
4. Place a saucepan over medium heat. Heat in it the milk for few minutes. Turn off the heat and mix into it the sour cream.
5. Place it aside to cool down completely.
6. Get a large mixing bowl: Cream in it the 1/2 C. granulated sugar, eggs, and egg yolks until they become pale.
7. Mix in the milk and cream mix with yeast mix, 1 tsp of almond extract, and a pinch of salt.
8. Add to it 5 1/2 C. of flour gradually while mixing them all the time until you get a soft dough.

9. Transfer the dough to a floured surface. Knead it for 6 min while adding to it the remaining flour gradually.

10. Place the dough in a greased bowl and cover it with a wet towel. Let it rise for 11 min.

11. Once the time is up, add cranberry mixture, raisins, and almonds. knead them until it are included in the dough.

12. Press the dough into an 8 inches circle. Poke the middle of it with the back of a spoon then pull it until it becomes 2 inches.

13. Lay the dough gently in the greased Bundt pan. Cover the dough pan with a wet towel and let it rise for 46 min.

14. Once the time is up, place the cake in the oven and cook it for 46 min.

15. To make the Icing:

16. Get a mixing bowl: Whisk in it the powdered sugar, 1/4 C. milk, and 1/4 tsp almond extract until they become smooth.

17. Allow the cake to cool down completely. Garnish it with the icing then serve it with your favorite toppings.

18. Enjoy.

GOLDEN
Carrots

 Prep Time: 20 mins
Total Time: 1 hr 5 mins

Servings per Recipe: 4
Calories   106.3
Fat   6.0g
Cholesterol   15.2mg
Sodium   119.4mg
Carbohydrates   12.9g
Protein   1.2g

Ingredients

1 lb. carrot, cut into sticks
2 tbsp butter
1 tsp sugar

2 tsp flour
salt

Directions

1. Place the carrots with butter in a large saucepan. Cover it with boiling water and a pinch of salt.
2. Let it cook over low heat for 35 min.
3. Get a small mixing bowl: Mix in it the flour with 1 tbsp of butter.
4. Stir it into the carrots and cook them for 3 min. Stir in the sugar next and cook them until they start boiling.
5. Let them cook for 7 to 12 min. Serve it warm.
6. Enjoy.

Sweet
Nigella Bread

🥣 Prep Time: 15 mins

🕐 Total Time: 1 hr 15 mins

Servings per Recipe: 16

Calories	160.7
Fat	3.8g
Cholesterol	0.0mg
Sodium	292.3mg
Carbohydrates	28.1g
Protein	3.6g

Ingredients

1 1/4 C. warm water
2 tbsp honey, dark
1/4 C. olive oil
3 C. bread flour
1 1/2 C. rye flour
2 tsp salt

2 tsp fast rising yeast
1/2 tbsp nigella seeds
1/3 C. dried cranberries
1 tbsp caraway seed

Directions

1. Combine the water with honey, oil, flours, yeast, and salt in a bread machine.
2. Press the dough cycle button. When the bread machine beeps, add to it the caraways seeds and nigella seeds.
3. Grease a baking sheet.
4. When the cycle is done, shape the dough into 2 halves. Place them in the baking sheet.
5. Cover the loaves with a wet kitchen towel and let them rest for 60 min.
6. Before you do anything, preheat the oven to 350 F.
7. Coat the loaves with egg. Cook them in the oven for 60 min.
8. Allow the bread loaves to cool down completely then serve them.
9. Enjoy.

ELECTRIC
Buckwheat Cream Bread

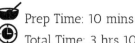 Prep Time: 10 mins

Total Time: 3 hrs 10 mins

Servings per Recipe: 1

Calories	2342.2
Fat	82.0g
Cholesterol	425.6mg
Sodium	1876.5mg
Carbohydrates	343.6g
Protein	59.7g

Ingredients

2 1/4 tsp active dry yeast
2 2/3 C. bread flour
3/4 C. buckwheat flour
3/4 tsp salt
1 1/2 tbsp sugar
1 egg

1 egg yolk
1/4 C. sour cream
1/4 C. vegetable oil
3/4 C. water

Directions

1. Combine all the ingredients in the bread machine.
2. Follow the instructions of the manufacturer to cook it.
3. Allow the bread loaf to cool down completely then serve it.
4. Enjoy.

Cottage
Carrot Pie

Prep Time: 15 mins
Total Time: 1 hr

Servings per Recipe: 6
Calories   174.9
Fat   9.4g
Cholesterol   55.1mg
Sodium   502.2mg
Carbohydrates   14.7g
Protein   9.0g

Ingredients

3 tbsp butter
1 C. minced onion
1/2 tsp salt
1 lb. carrot, peeled, sliced
1 tbsp flour
1 1/2 C. cottage cheese
1/2 C. grated mild white cheese

1 egg, beaten
lots ground black pepper
1 tbsp dried dill weed
3 tbsp wheat germ
paprika

Directions

1. Before you do anything, preheat the oven to 375 F. Grease a baking pan.
2. Place a large pan over medium heat. Melt in it the butter. Cook in it the onion with a pinch of salt for 5 min.
3. Stir in the carrots with a pinch of salt. Put on the lid and let them cook for 6 min until the carrots become soft.
4. Add the flour and mix them well.
5. Get a mixing bowl: Cream in it the egg with cheese. Add the carrot mix with dill, a pinch of salt and pepper.
6. Mix them well. Spoon the mixture into the pie shell. Place it in the oven and cook it for 16 min.
7. Once the time is up, lower the oven heat to 350 F. Let the pie cook for an extra 32 min.
8. Allow the pie to cool down for a while then serve it with your favorite toppings.
9. Enjoy.

BLACK TIE
Cake

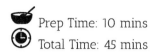 Prep Time: 10 mins
Total Time: 45 mins

Servings per Recipe: 10
Calories	292.7
Fat	2.6g
Cholesterol	75.8mg
Sodium	119.2mg
Carbohydrates	61.7g
Protein	6.5g

Ingredients

4 eggs
1 C. plain low-fat yogurt
2 C. sugar
2 C. all-purpose flour

2 tsp baking powder
2 tbsp cocoa powder

Directions

1. Before you do anything, preheat the oven to 350 F. Grease a baking pan.
2. Get a mixing bowl: Beat in it eggs, yogurt and sugar.
3. Add to it the flour with baking powder. Mix them well.
4. Divide the mixture into 2 portions. Add to one batter portion the cocoa powder and mix them well.
5. Place 1 tbsp of the white batter in the middle of the pan. Pour over it 1 tbsp of the chocolate batter.
6. Repeat the process by alternating between the white and chocolate batter.
7. Place the cake in the oven and let it cook for 32 to 36 min.
8. Allow the cake to cool down completely. Serve it with your favorite toppings.
9. Enjoy.

Smoked
Salmon Fritters

🥣 Prep Time: 10 mins
🕐 Total Time: 15 mins

Servings per Recipe: 4
Calories	576.6
Fat	30.2g
Cholesterol	202.0mg
Sodium	611.3mg
Carbohydrates	51.7g
Protein	26.1g

Ingredients

1 C. buckwheat flour
1 C. all-purpose flour
1 pinch salt
1 tbsp fast rise yeast
2 eggs
1 1/2 C. milk, warm
2 tbsp unsalted butter, melted

2/3 C. crème fraiche
3 tbsp dill, chopped
8 oz. smoked salmon, sliced

Directions

1. Get a mixing bowl: Stir in it the buckwheat, flour and salt with yeast.
2. Get a mixing bowl: Whisk in it 2 egg yolks with 1 egg white, warm milk and 1 tbsp of melted butter.
3. Add to them the flour mixture and mix them well until they make a smooth batter. Cover the bowl and place it in the fridge to rest for 1 h 30 min. Get a large mixing bowl: Beat in it the remaining egg white until it soft peaks.
4. Add it to the flour batter and stir it gently.
5. Place a large skillet over medium heat. Melt in it some butter. Use a tbsp to drop mound of the mixture in the hot pot skillet.
6. Cook the fritters for 1 min on each side until they become golden brown.
7. Get a mixing bowl: Mix in it the dill with crème fraiche, a pinch of salt and pepper.
8. Top the fritters with the smoked salmon. Drizzle over the crème fraiche sauce then serve them warm.
9. Enjoy.

BEEF
Meatballs with Catsup Sauce

Prep Time: 30 mins
Total Time: 1 hr 45 mins

Servings per Recipe: 8
Calories   154.9
Fat   6.7g
Cholesterol   63.3mg
Sodium   646.6mg
Carbohydrates   10.5g
Protein   13.4g

Ingredients

1 lb. lean ground beef
1 egg
1/2 tsp salt
1/2 tsp chili powder
1/4 C. catsup
1/2 C. fine cracker crumb
1 (10 1/2 oz.) cans tomato soup
2 C. water
1 tsp chili powder
1/4 tsp salt
1 large onion, chopped

1 medium green pepper, chopped
2 - 3 garlic cloves, chopped
1 C. celery, chopped
1 bay leaf
1 beef bouillon cube

Directions

1. Before you do anything, preheat the oven to 350 F. Grease a baking pan.
2. Get a mixing bowl: Combine in it the beef, egg, 1/2 tsp salt, 1/2 tsp chili powder, catsup and cracker crumbs.
3. Shape the mixture into bite size meatballs. Place them on a lined up baking sheet.
4. Place a large pot over medium heat. Stir in it the tomato soup with water, chili powder, onion, green pepper, garlic, celery, bay leaf, bouillon cube, and salt.
5. Cook them until they start boiling. Add the meatballs to the sauce. Let them cook for 4 min.
6. Put on the lid and transfer the pot to the oven. let it cook for 60 min.
7. Serve your saucy meatballs with some rice and noodles.
8. Enjoy.

Spicy Nuts Cake

Prep Time: 10 mins
Total Time: 15 mins

Servings per Recipe: 8
Calories	176.3
Fat	4.2g
Cholesterol	0.0mg
Sodium	205.2mg
Carbohydrates	36.0g
Protein	3.5g

Ingredients

1 C. whole wheat flour
1/2 C. oat bran, uncooked
1 tsp baking powder
1 tsp baking soda
1/2 tsp ground nutmeg
1/4 tsp ground cloves
1/4 raisins
2 tbsp chopped walnuts

1/2 C. honey
1/2 C. unsweetened applesauce
1/2 C. orange juice
1 tbsp vegetable oil
1 tsp vegetable oil
salt

Directions

1. Before you do anything, preheat the oven to 350 F. Grease a baking loaf pan.
2. Get a mixing bowl: Mix in it the flour, oat bran, baking powder, baking soda, raisins, walnuts, salt and spices.
3. Get a small mixing bowl: Whisk in it the applesauce with oils and orange juice.
4. Add them to the flour mix and combine them until they become smooth.
5. Pour the batter into the greased pan. Place it in the oven and let it cook for 36 min.
6. Allow the cake to cool down completely then serve it with your favorite toppings.
7. Enjoy.

EASY
Wienerschnitzel

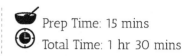 Prep Time: 15 mins
Total Time: 1 hr 30 mins

Servings per Recipe: 4	
Calories	515 kcal
Fat	29.1 g
Carbohydrates	33.7g
Protein	29.1 g
Cholesterol	230 mg
Sodium	782 mg

Ingredients

1 1/2 lbs veal cutlets, flattened to 1/4
inch thickness
1/2 C. all-purpose flour
3 tbsps grated Parmesan cheese
2 eggs
1 tsp minced parsley
1/2 tsp salt
1/4 tsp pepper

1 pinch ground nutmeg
2 tbsps milk
1 C. dry bread crumbs
6 tbsps butter
4 slices lemon

Directions

1. Get a bowl, combine: milk, parmesan, nutmeg, eggs, pepper, parsley, and salt.
2. Get a 2nd bowl for your bread crumbs and 3rd bowl for your flour.
3. Coat your cutlets with flour first, then egg, and then the bread crumbs.
4. Layer all the cutlets in a dish and place everything in the fridge for 65 mins with a covering.
5. Sauté each piece in butter for 4 mins per side and then top the contents with drippings and a few pieces of lemon.
6. Enjoy.

Eastern European Style Lasagna

Prep Time: 10 mins

Total Time: 1 hr

Servings per Recipe: 12

Calories	303 kcal
Fat	17.6 g
Carbohydrates	22.1g
Protein	14.4 g
Cholesterol	42 mg
Sodium	1115 mg

Ingredients

9 lasagna noodles
1 (10.75 oz.) can condensed cream of mushroom soup
1 (10.75 oz.) can condensed cream of chicken soup
2 C. milk

1 lb kielbasa, cut in half, diced
1 (20 oz.) can sauerkraut, drained
8 oz. shredded mozzarella cheese

Directions

1. Set your oven to 375 degrees before doing anything else.
2. Boil your pasta in water and salt for 9 mins. Then remove all the liquids.
3. Now blend until smooth: milk, chicken soup, and mushrooms.
4. Layer the following in a casserole dish: 3 noodles, 1 C. soup, half sauerkraut, half of your sausage, and half of the cheese.
5. Continue layering until all of the ingredients have been used.
6. End with noodles if possible.
7. Now place a covering of foil around the dish and cook everything in the oven for 30 mins. Take off the foil and continue cooking the contents for 20 more mins. Now top everything with some cheese and let it melt outside the oven.
8. Enjoy.

STOVETOP
Egg Noodles

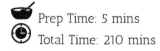

Prep Time: 5 mins
Total Time: 210 mins

Servings per Recipe: 4
Calories   690 kcal
Fat   28.2 g
Carbohydrates   93g
Protein   19 g
Cholesterol   155 mg
Sodium   325 mg

Ingredients

1 (16 oz.) package egg noodles
1 stick butter
1 medium head green cabbage, chopped

salt and pepper to taste

Directions

1. Boil your noodles in water and salt for 6 mins then remove all the liquids.
2. Simultaneously stir fry your cabbage in butter, then add some pepper and salt.
3. Fry this mix for 8 mins then combine in the noodles and the cabbage.
4. Continue cooking for 6 more mins.
5. Enjoy.

Lunch
in Germany

Prep Time: 15 mins
Total Time: 3 hrs 35 mins

Servings per Recipe: 12
Calories   777 kcal
Fat   62.3 g
Carbohydrates   28.6g
Protein   24.6 g
Cholesterol   128 mg
Sodium   2702 mg

Ingredients

2 lbs sauerkraut, rinsed and drained
1 tbsp caraway seeds (optional)
1/4 C. brown sugar
1 apple, diced
1/2 lb turkey bacon, cut into 1-inch pieces

1 large onion, chopped
1 1/2 lbs kielbasa sausage, cut into 1-inch thick slices

Directions

1. Get the following boiling: apples, sauerkraut, sugar, and caraway.
2. Once it is all boiling set the heat to low and let the contents cook for 120 min.
3. Stir the mix at least 3 or 4 times.
4. Coat a casserole dish with oil and then set your oven to 350 degrees before doing anything else.
5. Stir fry your onions and bacon for 12 mins then pour it into the sauerkraut mix.
6. Now stir fry your sausage in the drippings for 13 mins and add it in with the rest of the ingredients.
7. Layer everything into a baking dish and cook it all in the oven for 65 mins.
8. Enjoy.

ROASTED
BBQ Chicken with Sauerkraut

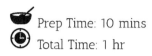

Prep Time: 10 mins
Total Time: 1 hr

Servings per Recipe: 4
Calories	253 kcal
Fat	1.9 g
Carbohydrates	29.2g
Protein	28.6 g
Cholesterol	68 mg
Sodium	1794 mg

Ingredients

4 skinless, boneless chicken breast halves
1 C. barbecue sauce

22 oz. sauerkrau

Directions

1. Set your oven to 350 degrees before doing anything else.
2. Pour your sauerkraut into a casserole dish and top it with the chicken pieces.
3. Now liberally add in your bbq sauce and cook the contents in the oven for 35 mins.
4. Enjoy.

Countryside
Cabbage

🍲 Prep Time: 10 mins
🕐 Total Time: 35 mins

Servings per Recipe: 6
Calories   568 kcal
Fat   46.2 g
Carbohydrates   22.2g
Protein   18.2 g
Cholesterol   75 mg
Sodium   1408 mg

Ingredients

1/2 C. margarine
1 onion, peeled and diced
1 head savoy cabbage, shredded
1 (15 oz.) can sliced potatoes
1 1/2 lbs kielbasa sausage
3 tbsps red wine vinegar

salt and pepper to taste
1/2 C. water

Directions

1. Stir fry your onions in margarine until tender. Then add the potatoes and the cabbage and cook the mix until the cabbage is soft.
2. Now add in: pepper, sausage, salt, wine, and vinegar.
3. Place a lid on the pot and continue cooking everything until the sausage is fully done.
4. Now add in your water and place the lid back on the pot again.
5. Cook the contents for 12 mins.
6. Enjoy.

CURRY
Sausage

Servings per Recipe: 4
Calories   451 kcal
Fat   31.7 g
Carbohydrates   26.1g
Protein   18.4 g
Cholesterol   75 mg
Sodium   3019 mg

Ingredients

3 (15 oz.) cans tomato sauce
1 lb kielbasa
2 tbsps chili sauce
1/2 tsp onion salt
1 tbsp white sugar

1 tsp ground black pepper
1 pinch paprika
Curry powder to taste

Directions

1. Turn on your oven's broiler before doing anything else.
2. Now get the following simmering with a low level of heat: pepper tomato sauce, sugar chili sauce, and onions salt.
3. Simmer this mix for 8 mins.
4. At the same time cook your sausage under the broiler for 5 mins per side. Then cut the sausage into half inch pieces.
5. Place your sausage pieces in a casserole dish and top them with the tomato sauce mix.
6. Now garnish everything with some curry powder and some paprika.
7. Enjoy.

Sour Cream and Onion Pie (Zwiebelkuchen)

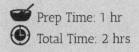 Prep Time: 1 hr
Total Time: 2 hrs

Servings per Recipe: 11
Calories   441 kcal
Fat   26.4 g
Carbohydrates   43.2g
Protein   10.3 g
Cholesterol   93 mg
Sodium   415 mg

Ingredients

6 lbs onions, sliced
4 slices turkey bacon
1 (16 oz.) container sour cream
4 egg
2 tbsps all-purpose flour
1/2 tsp salt
1/2 tsp caraway seed
2 recipes pastry for a 9 inch single crust pie

Directions

1. Set your oven to 425 degrees before doing anything else.
2. Layer your dough along a pizza pan.
3. Now stir fry your onions until see-through then put them in a bowl.
4. Stir fry your bacon, crumble it and add it with the onions.
5. Whisk your eggs and add them to the mix with the sour cream and salt as well.
6. Stir everything and then add flour.
7. Layer the contents on your dough and top the mix with some caraway.
8. Cook the contents for 65 mins in the oven.
9. Enjoy..

APPLES, Pickled Cabbage, and Sausage

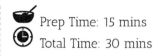
Prep Time: 15 mins
Total Time: 30 mins

Servings per Recipe: 6
Calories	591 kcal
Fat	41.7 g
Carbohydrates	35.7g
Protein	20.3 g
Cholesterol	100 mg
Sodium	2372 mg

Ingredients

6 apples - peeled, cored and chopped
1 (32 oz.) package sauerkraut
1/4 C. brown sugar

2 lbs kielbasa sausage, sliced

Directions

1. Get your sauerkraut boiling then add in your apples and continue gently boiling with a medium to low level of heat for 12 mins.
2. Now add in the sausage and the sugar and cook the mix for 7 more mins.
3. Enjoy.

German Style
Salad Dressing

Prep Time: 10 mins
Total Time: 15 mins

Servings per Recipe: 6
Calories	95 kcal
Fat	7 g
Carbohydrates	7.4g
Protein	1.2 g
Cholesterol	52 mg
Sodium	66 mg

Ingredients

1 egg yolk
3 tbsps white sugar
1 tbsp prepared mustard
2 tbsps butter

1/2 C. white vinegar
1/2 C. half-and-half

Directions

1. Get the following boiling: vinegar, egg yolk, butter, sugar, and mustard.
2. Continue boiling until it becomes thick. Once it has thickened shut the heat and add in the half and half.
3. Mix everything then place it all in the fridge until chilled.
4. Enjoy over salad.

GERMAN
Rump Roast

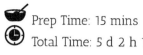 Prep Time: 15 mins

Total Time: 5 d 2 h 15m

Servings per Recipe: 6	
Calories	941 kcal
Fat	61.4 g
Carbohydrates	21.6g
Protein	69.2 g
Cholesterol	1224 mg
Sodium	1457 mg

Ingredients

2 C. cider vinegar
2 C. water
1/3 C. brown sugar
1/2 tsp ground cloves
1/2 tsp ground allspice
1 tbsp salt
1/2 tsp ground black pepper
6 black peppercorns

1 bay leaf
2 onions, diced
3 carrots, chopped
2 stalks celery, chopped
4 1/2 lbs rump roast
2 tbsps vegetable oil
1 C. sour cream

Directions

1. Get the following lightly simmer for 3 mins: celery, vinegar, carrots, water, onions, sugar, bay leaf, cloves, peppercorns, allspice, salt, and pepper.
2. Take your roast and create some holes in it.
3. Then place the roast in a bowl and top it with the wet mix.
4. Place a lid on the bowl and let it sit in the fridge for at least 4 days. Make sure you flip the roast 1 time each day.
5. Now separate the roast from the marinade.
6. Take the marinade and separate the liquid from the veggies with a strainer. Keep both separate.
7. But throw away the peppercorns.
8. Sear your roast, all over, in hot oil, in a Dutch oven for 2 to 3 mins per side.
9. Set the heat to low and pour in the veggies and 1 C. of liquid.
10. Place a lid on the pot and let it all cook over low heat for 90 mins. If all the liquid cooks out add more in.
11. Now take out your roast and carve it.
12. Then put the pieces back in the liquid.

13. Place the lid back on the pot and cook everything for 35 more mins.
14. Set the meat to the side and add some sour cream to the liquid and get it hot while stirring for 2 mins.
15. Top the roast with the drippings.
16. Enjoy.

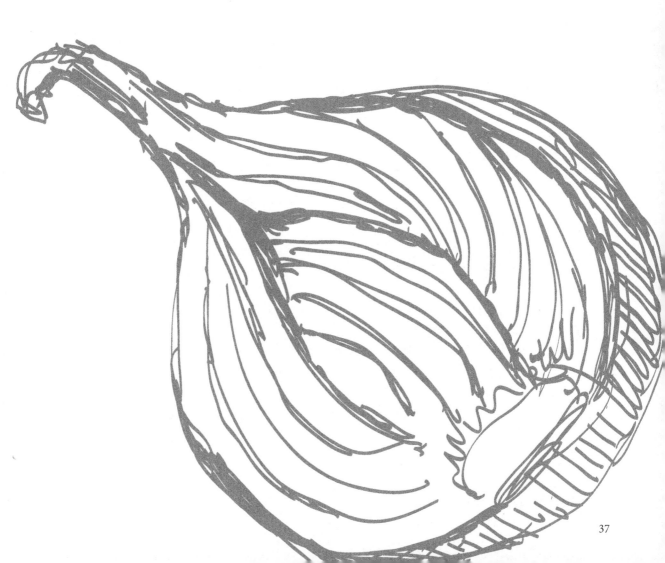

GERMAN STYLE
Soup I

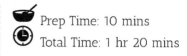 Prep Time: 10 mins
Total Time: 1 hr 20 mins

Servings per Recipe: 12
Calories	327 kcal
Fat	22.4 g
Carbohydrates	20.6g
Protein	11.6 g
Cholesterol	32 mg
Sodium	1377 mg

Ingredients

4 C. water
2 1/2 C. chicken broth
4 tbsps chicken soup base
1/2 tsp ground black pepper
2 large carrots, finely chopped
4 potatoes, peeled and diced
1 large onion, diced
2 stalks celery, finely chopped
1 red bell pepper, diced
1 C. mayonnaise

8 oz. processed cheese food (eg. Velveeta)
1 C. shredded sharp Cheddar cheese
1/2 C. shredded Swiss cheese
1/4 C. dry potato flakes

Directions

1. Get the following boiling: water, onions, broth, potatoes, chicken soup base, carrots, and black pepper.
2. Once it is boiling set the heat to low and cook the mix for 17 mins.
3. Stir every 5 mins. Add in the celery and the bell peppers and cook this for 7 more mins. Now add the mayo and stir everything until smooth. Add all the cheese slowly, while whisking, until it is all melted.
4. Cook the mix for about 4 to 6 more mins, while stirring, and then add the potato flakes.
5. Shut the heat and wait for 17 mins before plating the dish. Enjoy.

Bavarian Chocolate Cheese Truffles

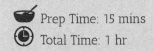

Prep Time: 15 mins
Total Time: 1 hr

Servings per Recipe: 24
Calories   224.9
Fat   11.9g
Cholesterol   15.5mg
Sodium   256.4mg
Carbohydrates   28.5g
Protein   3.0g

Ingredients

1 (18 1/4 oz.) boxes chocolate cake mix
2 (3 oz.) boxes raspberry Jell-O gelatin
12 oz. cream cheese, room temp
1 (12 oz.) frozen whipped topping, thawed and divided

1/4 C. frozen raspberries
1/4 C. granulated sugar

Directions

1. Set your oven to 350 degrees F before doing anything else and grease and flour 11x15-inch jelly roll pans.
2. Prepare the cake mix according to package's instructions.
3. Divide the cake mixture into the prepared pans evenly and with the back of a spatula, smooth the surface.
4. Cook in the oven for about 15 minutes or till a toothpick inserted in the center of cakes comes out clean.Remove from the oven and keep onto the wire rack to cool in the pan for about 5-10 minutes.
5. Carefully, invert the cakes onto the wire rack to cool completely.
6. In a bowl, dissolve the gelatin into 1 2/3 C. of the boiling water and keep aside for about 2 minutes. In a food processor, add the cream cheese and pulse for about 1 minute.
7. Add the gelatin mixture and pulse for about 1 minute.
8. Transfer the gelatin mixture into a large bowl.
9. With a rubber spatula, gently fold in 4 C. of the whipped topping.
10. Place the gelatin mixture over each cake evenly and refrigerate to chill for about 15 minute. Place 1 cake layer over second cake layer.
11. Spread remaining whipped topping on top of the cake evenly.
12. In a bowl, add the granulated sugar and roll the frozen raspberries in it.
13. Cut the cake into equal sized squares and top with the raspberries.

BAVARIAN
Veggie Soup

Prep Time: 20 mins
Total Time: 1 hr 20 mins

Servings per Recipe: 8
Calories	187.4
Fat	9.0g
Cholesterol	22.9mg
Sodium	48.3mg
Carbohydrates	25.2g
Protein	3.9g

Ingredients

6 tbsp unsalted butter
4 carrots, cut into 3/8 inch thick rounds
salt & freshly ground black pepper
1/4 C. finely chopped fresh parsley leaves
1 large celery root, peeled and sliced 1/4 inch thick
1 parsley root, peeled and sliced 1/4 inch thick
4 leeks, split lengthwise, washed well, and sliced
1 small cauliflower, broken into florets

1/2 lb. sugar snap pea, tough strings removed
1/2 lb. green beans, ends trimmed and cut into 1 inch pieces
1/2 head savoy cabbage, damaged outer leaves discarded, cored, and thinly sliced
1 lb. potato, peeled and sliced 1/4 inch thick
1 1/2 C. water

Directions

1. In a large casserole, melt 3 tbsp of the butter on medium-high heat and remove from the heat.
2. In the bottom of the casserole, arrange the carrots in a layer and sprinkle with the salt, pepper and a little of the parsley.
3. Top with the layer of the celery root, followed by the layers of the parsley root, leeks, cauliflower florets, sugar snap pea, green beans, savoy cabbage and potato, sprinkling each layer with the salt, pepper and parsley.
4. Place the remaining 3 tbsp of the butter over the potatoes in the form of the dots.
5. Place the water over the vegetables.
6. Cover the casserole tightly and bring to a boil.
7. Reduce the heat to low and simmer for about 1 hour.

Bavarian
Coconut Truffles

🍳 Prep Time: 15 mins
🕐 Total Time: 8 hrs 15 mins

Servings per Recipe: 11
Calories	432.3
Fat	22.8g
Cholesterol	99.8mg
Sodium	139.5mg
Carbohydrates	52.6g
Protein	7.7g

Ingredients

1 1/2 tbsp gelatin
4 tbsp coconut milk
1 (14 oz.) cans sweetened condensed milk
1 C. coconut milk
1/2 C. sugar
4 egg yolks

1 crème fraîche, Alouette Cuisine
7 oz. shredded coconut (toasted)

Directions

1. In a bowl, dissolve the gelatin into 4 tbsp of the coconut milk. Keep aside to bloom. In a pan, add the condensed milk and remaining coconut milk on medium-high heat and bring to a gentle boil.
2. In a bowl, add the sugar and egg yolks and beat well.
3. Add a small amount the hot milk mixture into the egg yolk mixture and beat well. Slowly, add the egg yolk mixture into the milk mixture and cook for about 5-7 minutes, stirring continuously.
4. Remove from the heat and stir in the gelatin mixture.
5. Transfer the mixture into a bowl and refrigerate till the mixture begins to gel.
6. In another bowl, add the crème fraîche and beat till soft peaks form.
7. In the bowl of gel mixture, fold in crème fraiche.
8. Immediately, place the mixture into your favorite molds and refrigerate overnight.
9. Remove from the molds and serve with a topping of the shredded coconut.

BAVARIAN
Swedish Meatball

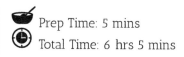

Prep Time: 5 mins
Total Time: 6 hrs 5 mins

Servings per Recipe: 10
Calories   40.6
Fat   0.0g
Cholesterol   0.0mg
Sodium   3.4mg
Carbohydrates   7.6g
Protein   0.2g

Ingredients

1 (6 -8 oz.) bags frozen precooked
meatballs, thawed
1 medium onion, sliced
1/4 C. brown sugar, packed

3 tbsp beef and onion soup mix
1 (12 oz.) bottles beer, optional

Directions

1. In a slow cooker, add all the ingredients and gently, stir to combine.
2. Set the crock pot on Low and cook, covered for about 5-6 hours.
3. Serve immediately.

Beef Rolls
of Bacon, Onions, and Pickles (Rouladen Bavarian)

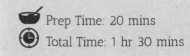 Prep Time: 20 mins

Total Time: 1 hr 30 mins

Servings per Recipe: 6
Calories	264 kcal
Fat	17.4 g
Carbohydrates	7.7g
Protein	19.1 g
Cholesterol	59 mg
Sodium	1450 mg

Ingredients

1 1/2 lbs flank steak, 1/4 inch fillets, 3 inches in width
German stone ground mustard, to taste
1/2 lb thick sliced turkey bacon
2 large onions, sliced
1 (16 oz.) jar dill pickle slices

2 tbsps butter
2 1/2 C. water
1 cube beef bouillon

Directions

1. Top each piece of steak with mustard then layer: onions, pickles, and bacon on each.
2. Shape the filet into a roll then place a toothpick in each to preserve the structure.
3. Brown your steaks in butter then add in 2.5 C. of water and bouillon.
4. Mix the bouillon and water together and then gently boil the rolls for 60 mins with a low level of heat.
5. Enjoy.

BAVARIAN
Empanadas

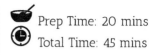
Prep Time: 20 mins
Total Time: 45 mins

Servings per Recipe: 6

Calories	674 kcal
Fat	42.3 g
Carbohydrates	32.5g
Protein	37.1 g
Cholesterol	114 mg
Sodium	894 mg

Ingredients

1/2 C. chopped onion
1 1/2 lbs lean ground beef
1 (16 oz.) can sauerkraut, drained and
pressed dry

2 (8 oz.) cans refrigerated crescent rolls
1 (8 oz.) package shredded Cheddar
cheese

Directions

1. Set your oven to 350 degrees before doing anything else.
2. Stir fry your beef and onions until the beef is fully done then remove all the excess oils before adding in your sauerkraut.
3. Get everything hot and then shut the heat.
4. Flatten your rolls and then place them into a casserole dish.
5. Top the rolls with the onion mix and then layer the 2nd piece of dough on top.
6. Crimp the edges of the two layers of dough together then top everything with some cheese.
7. Cook the dish in the oven for 27 mins.
8. Enjoy.

London
Roast

🥣 Prep Time: 20 mins

🕐 Total Time: 3 hrs 20 mins

Servings per Recipe: 6

Calories	547 kcal
Fat	31 g
Carbohydrates	2.3g
Protein	61.2 g
Cholesterol	184 mg
Sodium	255 mg

Ingredients

5 lbs beef round roast
salt and pepper to taste
2 tbsps butter
1/2 C. water
1/2 tsp dried sage
1/2 tsp dried mint
1 medium onion, sliced (optional)
1 clove garlic, minced (optional)
1/8 tsp seasoning salt (optional)

1/8 tsp red pepper flakes (optional)
1 tbsp butter
1 tbsp all-purpose flour
1/2 C. cold water
1/4 tsp dried sage
1/4 tsp dried mint

Directions

1. Set your oven to 350 degrees before doing anything else.
2. Brown your beef in a large pot in 2 tbsps of butter after seasoning the meat with pepper and salt.
3. Now add half a C. of water and half a tsp of mint and sage. Add garlic, pepper flakes, and onions as well if you like. Now place a lid on the pot.
4. Cook everything in the oven for 3 hrs.
5. With flour and 1 tbsp of butter make a roux.
6. Shut off the heat and add in half a C. of cold water to the roux.
7. Mix everything evenly then turn the heat back on.
8. Add in the rest of your mint and sage and take the liquid from the beef and add this with the roux.
9. Simmer the contents until you have a thick gravy.
10. Enjoy your beef with the gravy.

ENGLISH
Fish Savory Pie of Salmon and Haddock

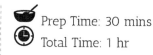

Prep Time: 30 mins
Total Time: 1 hr

Servings per Recipe: 6
Calories	695 kcal
Fat	26.4 g
Carbohydrates	58.8g
Protein	55 g
Cholesterol	148 mg
Sodium	1332 mg

Ingredients

1 tbsp olive oil
2 onions, halved and sliced
6 potatoes, peeled and cubed
2 C. frozen green peas
2 (6 oz.) salmon fillets, cut into 1 inch
cubes
1 lb smoked haddock fillets, undyed, cut
into 1 inch cubes
1 C. flaked or diced smoked salmon

1 tbsp butter
1 tbsp all-purpose flour
3 C. milk
1 1/2 C. Red Leicester cheese, grated
1 tsp ground nutmeg
1 tsp ground black pepper, or to taste
1/2 tsp salt

Directions

1. Coat a casserole dish with oil and then set your oven to 350 degrees before doing anything else.
2. Stir fry your onions for 10 mins in oil.
3. Boil your potatoes until soft in a separate pot. Then remove all the liquid and place the potatoes in a casserole dish.
4. Put the following in the dish as well: smoked salmon, onions, haddock, and regular salmon.
5. Now add some butter and flour to the same pot that the onions were fried in.
6. Cook and stir the contents to make a roux then add in your milk and get the contents lightly boiling. Stir and simmer until everything gets thick.
7. Finally add in your pepper, salt, and nutmeg. Add your cheese and stir until melted. Save a bit of cheese for a garnish later.
8. Cover your salmon with the new sauce. And add your remaining cheese.
9. Cook everything in the oven for 33 mins.
10. Enjoy.

British
Mushroom and Beef Skirt Steak

🥘 Prep Time: 20 mins
🕐 Total Time: 1 hr 5 mins

Servings per Recipe: 6
Calories	433 kcal
Fat	20.4 g
Carbohydrates	9.2g
Protein	39.8 g
Cholesterol	85 mg
Sodium	453 mg

Ingredients

9 fluid oz. red wine
1 onion, diced
2 cloves garlic, diced
1 sprig fresh thyme
2 tbsps butter
1 1/2 lbs beef skirt steak, cut into cubes

1 tbsp all-purpose flour
1 C. beef stock
salt and pepper to taste
9 oz. mixed wild mushrooms

Directions

1. Boil the following until 1/4 of it has evaporated: thyme, red wine, garlic, and onions. Then let it sit.
2. Stir fry your beef in butter until browned all over and then add it to the wet mix of wine.
3. Now add your flour to the same pan as the beef and with a low heat stir the mix until it gets slightly brown then slowly add your beef stock and keep stirring.
4. Get the contents boiling then add in your pepper and salt. Let this boil for 12 mins. Now add your wine and beef to the flour mix and place a lid on the pan and let the mix cook for 47 mins with a low heat.
5. Put the mushrooms over the beef and let the contents continue to lightly boil while covered.
6. Enjoy.

PROPER
Carrot Pudding

Prep Time: 20 mins
Total Time: 4 hrs 20 mins

Servings per Recipe: 12	
Calories	372 kcal
Fat	16.6 g
Carbohydrates	55.3g
Protein	3.7 g
Cholesterol	3 mg
Sodium	269 mg

Ingredients

1/2 C. shortening
1 C. white sugar
1 1/2 C. all-purpose flour
1 tsp baking soda
3/4 tsp salt
1 tsp ground cinnamon
1 tsp ground nutmeg
1/2 tsp ground cloves
1 C. grated carrots
1 C. raisins

1 C. diced walnuts
3/4 C. white sugar
1 1/2 tsps cornstarch
1 pinch salt
1 1/4 C. hot water
3 1/2 tsps butter
3 1/2 tsps lemon juice
1 1/2 tsps vanilla extract

Directions

1. Get a bowl, mix: 1 C. of sugar and shortening. Then add: cloves, flour, nutmeg, baking soda, cinnamon, and salt. Mix everything nicely.
2. Now add: walnuts, raisins and carrots. Put everything in an oiled pudding mold.
3. Wrap foil around the mold. Get a Dutch oven and pour in about 3 inches of water then put the mold inside the pot as well.
4. Place a lid on the pot and get the water boiling. Lower the heat to a light simmer and let it cook for 4.5 hours.
5. To make a lemon topping add the following to a large pan: salt, 3/4 C. of sugar, and cornstarch.
6. Add in vanilla, hot water, lemon juice, and butter.
7. Warm everything with a low to medium level of heating until it becomes a glaze.
8. Now put your pudding in a storage container or a bowl and before eating it garnish the pudding with some lemon topping.
9. Enjoy.

English Style
Cheddar Beef Hash

🥣 Prep Time: 30 mins
🕐 Total Time: 1 hr 15 mins

Servings per Recipe: 6
Calories	447 kcal
Fat	12.7 g
Carbohydrates	59.1g
Protein	26.6 g
Cholesterol	60 mg
Sodium	910 mg

Ingredients

4 large baking potatoes, peeled and cubed
1 (16 oz.) can baked beans
1 (12 oz.) can corned beef, sliced equal pieces

1 dash Worcestershire sauce
1/2 C. shredded sharp Cheddar cheese

Directions

1. Set your oven to 400 degrees before doing anything else.
2. Boil your potatoes in water for 13 mins. The remove all the water and add the following to them: salt, butter, and milk. Now mash the potatoes and then add some salt.
3. Get a baking dish and line the bottom with your beans then a layer of corned beef, then some Worcestershire sauce and finally your potatoes.
4. Cook everything in the oven for 25 mins then add your cheese and cook for another 20 mins.
5. Enjoy.

CLASSICAL
Trifle III (Creamy Raspberry and Strawberry)

Prep Time: 30 mins
Total Time: 1 hr 30 mins

Servings per Recipe: 12	
Calories	432 kcal
Fat	23.5 g
Carbohydrates	51.7g
Protein	4.6 g
Cholesterol	86 mg
Sodium	305 mg

Ingredients

1/2 C. margarine
1/2 C. white sugar
2 eggs
1 3/4 C. all-purpose flour
1/2 tsp baking powder
1/2 tsp salt
1 pint heavy cream
1/4 C. white sugar
1 tsp vanilla extract
1 (4.6 oz.) package non-instant vanilla

pudding mix
1 (8 oz.) jar seedless raspberry jam
1/2 C. sherry
4 fresh peaches - peeled, pitted, and sliced
1 pint fresh strawberries, rinsed and sliced
1 pint blueberries

Directions

1. Coat a cake pan with oil and then set your oven to 350 degrees before doing anything else.
2. Get a bowl, mix: half a C. of sugar, margarine, and eggs (one by one). Then add: salt, baking powder, and flour. Put everything in your cake pan after combining it all nicely.
3. Cook the mix in the oven for 25 mins. After the cake has cooled divide it into bite sized chunks 1 inch in width.
4. Get a 2nd bowl, mix the following until stiff: vanilla, cream, and one fourth C. of sugar.
5. Now make your pudding according to its instructions and put everything to the side.
6. Layer the bottom of a glass bowl or trifle dish with cake pieces that have a topping of jam.
7. Then half of the following: blueberries, strawberries, peaches, and pudding.
8. Finally put one third of the whipped cream. Continue the layering process until all ingredients have been used.
9. Let the contents get cold in the fridge before serving.
10. Enjoy.

British
Cottage Pie

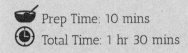 Prep Time: 10 mins
🕐 Total Time: 1 hr 30 mins

Servings per Recipe: 6
Calories	512 kcal
Fat	30.9 g
Carbohydrates	34.8g
Protein	24.1 g
Cholesterol	100 mg
Sodium	491 mg

Ingredients

1 lb lean ground beef
1 onion, diced
3 carrots, diced
2 tbsps all-purpose flour
1/2 tsp ground cinnamon
1 tbsp Italian seasoning
2 tbsps diced fresh parsley
1 1/2 C. beef broth
1 tbsp tomato paste
salt and pepper to taste

4 potatoes, peeled and diced
1/4 C. butter, softened
1 C. milk
salt and pepper to taste
1/4 lb shredded Cheddar cheese

Directions

1. Set your oven to 400 degrees before doing anything else.
2. Fry your beef, carrots, and onions for 7 mins until the beef is fully done. Add in the following to the beef: parsley, flour, herbs, and cinnamon. Get a bowl, mix: tomato paste and broth, pepper, and salt. Combine this wet mix with the beef. For 17 mins cook everything with a light simmer. Stir the contents every 3 mins. Enter the mix into a pie dish. Cook your potatoes in boiling water for 17 mins. Then remove all the liquid and mash them.
3. Add in your butter, salt, milk, pepper, or margarine. Mash everything again. Top with cheddar.
4. Cover your beef with these potatoes in the pie dish.
5. Cook everything in the oven for 30 mins.
6. Enjoy after letting the dish sit for 5 mins.

PORTUGUESA
House Stew

 Prep Time: 20 mins

Total Time: 1 hr 5 mins

Servings per Recipe: 6
Calories	359 kcal
Fat	21.8 g
Carbohydrates	15.6g
Protein	27.4 g
Cholesterol	42 mg
Sodium	600 mg

Ingredients

3 tbsps lime juice
1 tbsp ground cumin
1 tbsp paprika
2 tsps minced garlic
1 tsp salt
1 tsp ground black pepper
1 1/2 lbs tilapia fillets, cut into chunks
2 tbsps olive oil
2 onions, diced
4 large bell peppers, sliced

1 (16 oz.) can diced tomatoes, drained
1 (16 oz.) can coconut milk
1 bunch fresh cilantro, diced (optional)

Directions

1. Get a bowl, combine: tilapia, pepper, lime juice, salt, cumin, garlic, and paprika. Stir the contents to evenly coat the fish and then place everything in the fridge for 60 mins.

2. Now begin to fry your onions in olive oil for 3 mins then reduce the heat to a medium level. Add in the bell pepper, diced tomatoes, and seasoned fish. Cook the contents for 1 min then add the coconut milk. Place a lid on the pot and cook the contents for 20 mins with a medium heat.

3. Stir the mix at least 2 times then add the cilantro and cook everything for 7 more mins. Enjoy.

Easy
Portuguese Style Rice

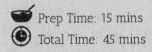 Prep Time: 15 mins
Total Time: 45 mins

Servings per Recipe: 6
Calories	201 kcal
Fat	3.7 g
Carbohydrates	37.5g
Protein	3.4 g
Cholesterol	0 mg
Sodium	297 mg

Ingredients

2 C. long-grain white rice, rinses and dried
2 tbsps minced onion
2 cloves garlic, minced

2 tbsps vegetable oil
1 tsp salt
4 C. hot water

Directions

1. Stir fry your onions in oil for 3 mins then add the garlic and cook the garlic until it is brown.
2. Now add the salt and the rice.
3. Toast the rice for a few mins until it is slightly browned then add the hot water.
4. Place a lid on the pot and cook the rice with a low level of heat for 23 mins.
5. Enjoy.

FRANGO
e Coconuts (Coconut Chicken)

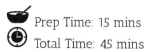

Prep Time: 15 mins
Total Time: 45 mins

Servings per Recipe: 4

Calories	345 kcal
Fat	19.9 g
Carbohydrates	11.5g
Protein	29.3 g
Cholesterol	72 mg
Sodium	234 mg

Ingredients

1 tsp ground cumin
1 tsp ground cayenne pepper
1 tsp ground turmeric
1 tsp ground coriander
4 skinless, boneless chicken breast halves
salt and pepper to taste
2 tbsps olive oil
1 onion, diced
1 tbsp minced fresh ginger

2 jalapeno peppers, seeded and diced
2 cloves garlic, minced
3 tomatoes, seeded and diced
1 (14 oz.) can light coconut milk
1 bunch diced fresh parsley

Directions

1. Get a bowl, combine: coriander, cumin, turmeric, and cayenne.
2. Now add in the chicken and also some pepper and salt.
3. Stir the contents to evenly coat the chicken pieces.
4. Now begin to stir fry your chicken in 1 tbsp of olive oil until fully done, for 16 mins.
5. Place the chicken to the side. Add in the rest of the oil and begin to fry the following for 7 mins: garlic, onion, jalapenos, and ginger.
6. Add the tomatoes and cook the mix for 10 more mins before pouring in the coconut milk.
7. Top the chicken with the tomato and coconut mix and then some parsley.
8. Enjoy.

Orange and Bean Soup

🥣 Prep Time: 30 mins
🕐 Total Time: 45 mins

Servings per Recipe: 6
Calories   80 kcal
Fat   2.7 g
Carbohydrates   13.3g
Protein   1.7 g
Cholesterol   0 mg
Sodium   788 mg

Ingredients

1 tbsp olive oil
3 C. onion, diced
8 cloves garlic, diced, divided
1 carrot, diced
3 tsps ground cumin
2 tsps salt
1 red bell pepper, diced

2 (15 oz.) cans black beans, drained and rinsed
1/2 C. water
1 C. orange juice
1 pinch cayenne pepper, or to taste

Directions

1. Stir fry your carrots, half of the garlic, and the onions in olive oil until soft. Then add in the salt and cumin.
2. Cook everything for 1 more min before adding in the red pepper and the rest of the garlic.
3. Cook the new garlic until it is soft.
4. Now add: orange juice, cayenne, water, and beans.
5. Now grab an immersion blender and puree the entire mix until it reaches a consistency you enjoy without any heating.
6. Heat everything back up after you have pureed it and continue cooking for 12 mins.
7. Enjoy.

PICADINHO'A
(Ground Beef Portuguese)

 Prep Time: 30 mins

Total Time: 2 hrs 10 mins

Servings per Recipe: 8
Calories	449 kcal
Fat	31.1 g
Carbohydrates	8g
Protein	25.2 g
Cholesterol	211 mg
Sodium	223 mg

Ingredients

1/2 C. olive oil
2 onions, diced
4 cloves diced garlic
2 lbs ground beef
3 stalks celery, diced
1 green bell pepper, diced
6 eggs
1 (15.5 oz.) can diced tomatoes, with liquid
1 C. diced fresh parsley

1 1/2 C. red wine
1/4 tsp crushed red pepper flakes, or to taste

Directions

1. Stir fry your garlic and onions in olive oil.
2. Cook them for 17 mins while constantly stirring.
3. At the same time get a bowl and mix: parsley, beef, tomatoes, celery, eggs, and bell pepper.
4. Combine the beef with the onions and turn up the heat.
5. Stir fry everything for 12 mins then set the heat to low and place a lid on the pot.
6. Cook the mix for 17 more mins then add the pepper flakes and the red wine.
7. Gently boil the contents with a low heat for 60 more mins.
8. Enjoy.

Banana and Coconut Bake

Prep Time: 15 mins
Total Time: 30 mins

Servings per Recipe: 6
Calories   135 kcal
Fat   3.9 g
Carbohydrates   26.2g
Protein   0.9 g
Cholesterol   5 mg
Sodium   56 mg

Ingredients

6 medium bananas, halved lengthwise
1/2 C. fresh orange juice
1 tbsp fresh lemon juice
1/2 C. white sugar

1/8 tsp salt
2 tbsps butter
1 C. flaked coconut

Directions

1. Coat a casserole dish with butter and then set your oven to 400 degrees before doing anything else.
2. Get a bowl, combine: salt, orange juice, sugar, and lemon juice.
3. Add the bananas to the casserole dish and top them with the lemon juice mix.
4. Now spread pieces of butter throughout.
5. Cook the bananas for 17 mins in the oven then garnish them with coconut.
6. Enjoy.

3-INGREDIENT
Ribs

 Prep Time: 10 mins
Total Time: 6 hrs 5 mins

Servings per Recipe: 3
Calories	698 kcal
Fat	56.5 g
Carbohydrates	0g
Protein	44.1 g
Cholesterol	163 mg
Sodium	3647 mg

Ingredients

1 (3 lb) rack of whole beef ribs, fat
removed
2 tbsps sea salt, or more if needed

3/4 C. water

Directions

1. Set your oven to 275 degrees before doing anything else.
2. Coat your beef with a generous amount of sea salt all over.
3. Then cook the meat in the oven for 6 hrs.
4. Baste the meat with beef broth after 60 mins has elapsed.
5. Continue basting every 60 mins. Then let the beef sit for 17 mins then cut it up.
6. Enjoy.

Easiest
Greek Chicken

Prep Time: 10 mins
Total Time: 8 hrs 30 mins

Servings per Recipe: 4
Calories   644 kcal
Fat   57.6 g
Carbohydrates   4g
Protein   27.8 g
Cholesterol   68 mg
Sodium   660 mg

Ingredients

4 skinless, boneless chicken breast halves
1 C. extra virgin olive oil
1 lemon, juiced
2 tsps crushed garlic
1 tsp salt

1 1/2 tsps black pepper
1/3 tsp paprika

Directions

1. Slice a few incisions into your pieces of chicken before doing anything else.
2. Now get a bowl, combine: paprika, olive oil, pepper, lemon juice, salt, and garlic.
3. Now add in the chicken and place the contents in the fridge for 8 hrs.
4. Grill your chicken until fully done with indirect heat on the side of the grill with the grilling grates oiled.
5. Enjoy.

PARSLEY
Pasta Salad

 Prep Time: 15 mins
Total Time: 2 hrs 30 mins

Servings per Recipe: 8
Calories   486 kcal
Fat   30.3 g
Carbohydrates   35.7g
Protein   19.8 g
Cholesterol   196 mg
Sodium   836 mg

Ingredients

2 (9 oz.) packages cheese tortellini
1/2 C. extra virgin olive oil
1/4 C. lemon juice
1/4 C. red wine vinegar
2 tbsps chopped fresh parsley
1 tsp dried oregano
1/2 tsp salt

6 eggs
1 lb. baby spinach leaves
1 C. crumbled feta cheese
1/2 C. slivered red onion

Directions

1. Boil your pasta in water and salt for 9 mins then remove all the liquids.
2. Get a bowl, mix: salt, olive oil, oregano, lemon juice, pasta, parsley, and vinegar.
3. Stir the contents and then place everything in the fridge for 3 hrs.
4. Get your eggs boiling in water, place a lid on the pot, and shut the heat.
5. Let the eggs stand for 15 mins. Then peel, and cut them into quarters.
6. Take out the bowl in the fridge and add in: onions, eggs, feta, and spinach.
7. Stir everything before serving.
8. Enjoy.

Orzo
Salad II

Prep Time: 15 mins
Total Time: 25 mins

Servings per Recipe: 6
Calories	329 kcal
Fat	19.6 g
Carbohydrates	28.1g
Protein	10.9 g
Cholesterol	37 mg
Sodium	614 mg

Ingredients

1 C. uncooked orzo pasta
1/4 C. pitted green olives
1 C. diced feta cheese
3 tbsps chopped fresh parsley
3 tbsps chopped fresh dill

1 ripe tomato, chopped
1/4 C. virgin olive oil
1/8 C. lemon juice
salt and pepper to taste

Directions

1. Cook your orzo in boiling water with salt for 9 mins.
2. Then remove the liquid and run the pasta under cool water.
3. Now get a bowl, combine: tomato, olive, dill, feta, parsley, and orzo.
4. Get a 2nd bowl, mix: lemon juice pepper, salt, and oil.
5. Combine both bowls and toss everything.
6. Place the mix in the fridge until cold.
7. Enjoy.

GREEK
Falafel

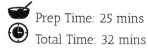

Prep Time: 25 mins
Total Time: 32 mins

Servings per Recipe: 6
Calories	317 kcal
Fat	16.8 g
Carbohydrates	35.2g
Protein	7.2 g
Cholesterol	0 mg
Sodium	724 mg

Ingredients

1 (19 oz.) can garbanzo beans, rinsed and drained
1 small onion, finely chopped
2 cloves garlic, minced
1 1/2 tbsps chopped fresh cilantro
1 tsp dried parsley
2 tsps ground cumin

1/8 tsp ground turmeric
1/2 tsp baking powder
1 C. fine dry bread crumbs
3/4 tsp salt
1/4 tsp cracked black peppercorns
1 quart vegetable oil for frying

Directions

1. Get a bowl, combine: pepper, onions, salt, garlic, bread crumbs, cilantro, baking powder, parsley, mashed garbanzos, turmeric, and cumin.
2. Form the contents into small balls and make about 20 of them.
3. Deep fry these falafels in hot oil until golden.
4. Enjoy.

Greek
Puff Pastry Bake II

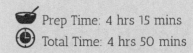

Prep Time: 4 hrs 15 mins
Total Time: 4 hrs 50 mins

Servings per Recipe: 4
Calories	515 kcal
Fat	32.6 g
Carbohydrates	33.6g
Protein	22.4 g
Cholesterol	101 mg
Sodium	524 mg

Ingredients

3 tbsps crushed garlic
1 egg yolk
2 C. chopped fresh spinach
2 boneless skinless chicken breast halves
2 tbsps basil pesto

1/3 C. chopped sun-dried tomatoes
1/4 C. crumbled herbed feta cheese
1 frozen puff pastry sheet, thawed, cut in half

Directions

1. Get a bowl, combine: egg yolks and garlic.
2. Add in the chicken and stir everything and before placing a lid on the bowl, and putting everything in the fridge for 5 hrs.
3. Coat a casserole dish with nonstick spray and then set your oven to 375 degrees before doing anything else.
4. Lay out half of your pastry on a cutting board covered with flour and add half a C. of spinach in the middle.
5. Place a piece of chicken on top of the spinach, then some pesto, half of the tomatoes, and half of feta.
6. Add the rest of the spinach and wrap the chicken with the pastry.
7. Crimp the edges of the pastry with your hands and put the pastry in the casserole dish.
8. Continue this process for all of your pieces of chicken.
9. Cook everything for 37 mins until the chicken is fully done.
10. Shut the heat to the oven and let the contents cool slightly before serving.
11. Enjoy.

CHICKEN
Souvlaki

Prep Time: 15 mins
Total Time: 2 hrs 30 mins

Servings per Recipe: 6

Calories	268 kcal
Fat	16.8 g
Carbohydrates	2.6 g
Protein	< 25.5 g
Cholesterol	71 mg
Sodium	295 mg

Ingredients

1/4 C. olive oil
2 tbsps lemon juice
2 cloves garlic, minced
1 tsp dried oregano
1/2 tsp salt
1 1/2 lbs skinless, boneless chicken breast halves - cut into bite-sized pieces
Sauce:
1 (6 oz.) container plain Greek-style yogurt
1/2 cucumber - peeled, seeded, and grated
1 tbsp olive oil
2 tsps white vinegar
1 clove garlic, minced
1 pinch salt
6 wooden skewers, or as needed

Directions

1. Take your skewers and submerge them in water before doing anything else.
2. Get a bowl, mix: half tsp salt, quarter of a C. of olive oil, chicken, oregano, lemon juice, and 2 cloves of garlic.
3. Place a covering on the bowl and put it all in the fridge for 3 hrs.
4. Get a 2nd bowl, combine: some salt, yogurt, 1 piece of garlic, 1 tbsp of olive oil, and the cucumbers. Place this in the fridge for 3 hrs as well. Stake your chicken on the skewers and then grill them for 9 mins, turn them over and cook for 8 more mins.
5. Top the chicken with the white sauce. Enjoy.

Greek Style
Minty Potato Bake

Prep Time: 20 mins
Total Time: 1 hr 40 mins

Servings per Recipe: 10
Calories	379 kcal
Fat	21.3 g
Carbohydrates	41g
Protein	8 g
Cholesterol	20 mg
Sodium	305 mg

Ingredients

5 lbs potatoes, cut into wedges
6 cloves garlic, minced
3/4 C. olive oil
1 C. water
1/4 C. fresh lemon juice
sea salt to taste

ground black pepper to taste
1 1/2 tbsps dried oregano
1 tsp chopped fresh mint
1 (8 oz.) package crumbled feta cheese

Directions

1. Coat a casserole dish with oil and then set your oven to 450 degrees before doing anything else.
2. Get a bowl, mix: pepper, potatoes, salt, garlic, lemon juice, water, and olive oil. Then layer everything in the dish.
3. Cook the contents for 45 mins then top the mix with mint and oregano.
4. Add some water (.5 C.) if the potatoes look too dry and cook everything for 42 more mins.
5. Now add some feta to the dish before letting the contents sit for 10 mins.
6. Enjoy.

EASY
Greek Dessert

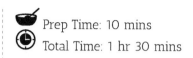 Prep Time: 10 mins
Total Time: 1 hr 30 mins

Servings per Recipe: 14
Calories	380 kcal
Fat	16.1 g
Carbohydrates	53.7g
Protein	6 g
Cholesterol	117 mg
Sodium	264 mg

Ingredients

3 C. cake flour
1 tsp baking soda
1/4 tsp salt
6 eggs, separated, egg whites in 1 bowl,
yolks in another
2 C. white sugar
1 C. butter, softened

2 tsps grated lemon zest
2 tbsps lemon juice
1 C. plain yogurt

Directions

1. Set your oven to 350 degrees before doing anything else.
2. Get a tube pan and coat it with oil and then set your oven to 350 degrees before doing anything else.
3. Whisk the egg whites until you find them peaking. Then slowly add in sugar (.5 C.) and keep whisking.
4. Get a 2nd bowl and whisk the following until airy: lemon juice, cream butter, lemon zest, 1.5 C. sugar, and the yolks.
5. Add in the egg whites and fill the tube pan with the mix.
6. Cook the contents for 55 mins. Then let the cake sit for 15 mins before slicing it.
7. Enjoy.

Mediterranean
Dijon Shrimp Salad

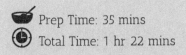 Prep Time: 35 mins

Total Time: 1 hr 22 mins

Servings per Recipe: 6

Calories	802 kcal
Fat	45.7 g
Carbohydrates	65.8g
Protein	33.6 g
Cholesterol	185 mg
Sodium	3398 mg

Ingredients

Dijon Vinaigrette:
1/4 C. rice wine vinegar
2 tbsps Dijon mustard
1 large clove garlic, minced
Big pinch of salt
Black pepper, to taste
2/3 C. extra-virgin olive oil
Pasta Salad:
2 medium zucchini, thinly sliced
lengthwise
1 medium yellow pepper, halved
lengthwise, seeded
2 tbsps olive oil

Ground black pepper and salt, to taste
1 gallon water
2 tbsps salt
1 lb. medium pasta shells
1 lb. cooked shrimp, halved lengthwise
8 oz. cherry tomatoes, halved
3/4 C. coarsely chopped, pitted Kalamata olives
1 C. crumbled feta cheese
1/2 small red onion, cut into small dice
2 tsps dried oregano

Directions

1. Combine the following in a jar, then shake: pepper, wine vinegar, salt, mustard, and garlic.
2. Coat your bell pepper and zucchini with olive oil (2 tbsps), pepper, and salt, then cook them under the broiler for 6 mins then flip them and broil for 5 more mins.
3. Place them in a bowl after dicing them.
4. Boil your pasta in water and salt for 9 mins then remove all the liquids.
5. Now mix the pasta, veggies, and dressing together in a bowl and stir the mix.
6. Enjoy.

GREEK
COUSCOUS

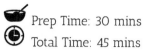 Prep Time: 30 mins
Total Time: 45 mins

Servings per Recipe: 20
Calories	159 kcal
Fat	6.5 g
Carbohydrates	21.4g
Protein	5.7 g
Cholesterol	10 mg
Sodium	642 mg

Ingredients

3 (6 oz.) packages garlic and herb couscous mix (or any flavor you prefer)
1 pint cherry tomatoes, cut in half
1 (5 oz.) jar pitted kalamata olives, halved
1 C. mixed bell peppers (green, red, yellow, orange), diced

1 cucumber, sliced and then halved
1/2 C. parsley, finely chopped
1 (8 oz.) package crumbled feta cheese
1/2 C. Greek vinaigrette salad dressing

Directions

1. Get your couscous boiling in water for 5 mins then place a lid on the pot, and let the grains sit in the water for 17 mins until all the liquid has been absorbed.
2. Add the couscous to a bowl with: feta, tomatoes, parsley, olives, cucumbers, and bell peppers.
3. Add in the dressing and stir the mix to evenly distribute the oils.
4. Enjoy.

Easy
Biscotti

Prep Time: 25 mins
Total Time: 1 hr 35 mins

Servings per Recipe: 30
Calories	138 kcal
Fat	7.8 g
Carbohydrates	15.5g
Protein	2.2 g
Cholesterol	25 mg
Sodium	89 mg

Ingredients

3/4 C. butter
1 C. white sugar
2 eggs
1 1/2 tsps vanilla extract
2 1/2 C. all-purpose flour
1 tsp ground cinnamon

3/4 tsp baking powder
1/2 tsp salt
1 C. hazelnuts

Directions

1. Coat a baking dish with oil then set your oven to 350 degrees before doing anything else.
2. Get a bowl, combine: sugar and butter. Mix the contents until it is creamy.
3. Now add in the vanilla and the eggs. Stir the mix then sift in: salt, flour, baking powder, and cinnamon. Stir everything again then add in the hazelnuts.
4. Now form your dough into 2 foot long cylinders.
5. Lay the cylinders on the cookie sheet and flatten them.
6. Let the dough cook in the oven for 35 mins. Then let the loaves lose their heat.
7. Now cut each one diagonally and place everything back in the oven for 12 more mins. Flip the loaves after 6 mins of cooking. Enjoy.

ITALIAN
Tuscan Soup

Prep Time: 15 mins
Total Time: 1 hr 10 mins

Servings per Recipe: 20	
Calories	459 kcal
Fat	34.1 g
Carbohydrates	21.1g
Protein	17.2 g
Cholesterol	87 mg
Sodium	1925 mg

Ingredients

1 (16 oz.) package smoked sausage
2 potatoes, cut into 1/4-inch slices
3/4 C. diced onion
6 slices turkey bacon
1 1/2 tsps minced garlic
2 C. kale - washed, dried, and shredded

2 tbsps chicken bouillon powder
1 quart water
1/3 C. heavy whipping cream

Directions

1. Set your oven to 300 degrees before doing anything else.
2. Place your pieces of sausage on a cookie sheet and cook everything in the oven for 30 mins.
3. Then divide the meat in half and then cut them in half again diagonally.
4. Begin to stir fry your bacon and onions until the onions are translucent then remove the bacon from the pan.
5. Add in the garlic and cook everything for 2 more mins then add the chicken base, potatoes, and water.
6. Let the mix gently boil for 20 mins then add in: the cream, bacon, kale, and sausage.
7. Let the soup cook for 5 mins.
8. Enjoy.

Chicken
Marsala Classicoi

Prep Time: 10 mins
Total Time: 30 mins

Servings per Recipe: 4
Calories	448 kcal
Fat	26.6 g
Carbohydrates	13.3g
Protein	28.8 g
Cholesterol	99 mg
Sodium	543 mg

Ingredients

1/4 C. all-purpose flour for coating
1/2 tsp salt
1/4 tsp ground black pepper
1/2 tsp dried oregano
4 skinless, boneless chicken breast halves
– flattened to 1/4 inch thick
4 tbsps butter

4 tbsps olive oil
1 C. sliced mushrooms
1/2 C. Marsala wine
1/4 C. cooking sherry

Directions

1. Get a bowl, combine: oregano, flour, pepper, and salt.
2. Dredge your pieces of chicken in the mix then begin to stir fry the chicken in butter.
3. Let the chicken fry until it is browned all over then add in: the sherry, mushrooms, and wine.
4. Place a lid on the pan and let the contents gently boil for 12 mins.
5. Enjoy.

MAGGIE'S
Easy Bruschetta

Prep Time: 15 mins
Total Time: 35 mins

Servings per Recipe: 12
Calories   215 kcal
Fat   8.9 g
Carbohydrates   24.8g
Protein   9.6 g
Cholesterol   12 mg
Sodium   426 mg

Ingredients

6 roma (plum) tomatoes, diced
1/2 C. sun-dried tomatoes, packed in oil
3 cloves minced garlic
1/4 C. olive oil
2 tbsps balsamic vinegar
1/4 C. fresh basil, stems removed

1/4 tsp salt
1/4 tsp ground black pepper
1 French baguette
2 C. shredded mozzarella cheese

Directions

1. Get your oven's broiler hot before doing anything else.
2. Now grab a bowl, mix: pepper, roma tomatoes, salt, sun-dried tomatoes, basil, garlic, vinegar, and olive oil.
3. Let this mix sit for 12 mins and begin to slice your bread into 3/4 of inch pieces.
4. Place the pieces of bread on a cookie sheet then place everything under the broiler for 3 mins.
5. Now evenly top each piece of bread with the roma tomato mix.
6. Then add a piece of cheese on top of each one.
7. Cook the bread slices under the broiler for 6 more mins.

Authentic
Eggplant Parmesan

🥣 Prep Time: 25 mins
🕐 Total Time: 1 hr

Servings per Recipe: 10
Calories	487 kcal
Fat	16 g
Carbohydrates	62.1g
Protein	24.2 g
Cholesterol	73 mg
Sodium	1663 mg

Ingredients

3 eggplant, peeled and thinly sliced
2 eggs, beaten
4 C. Italian seasoned bread crumbs
6 C. spaghetti sauce, divided
1 (16 oz.) package mozzarella cheese, shredded and divided

1/2 C. grated Parmesan cheese, divided
1/2 tsp dried basil

Directions

1. Set your oven to 350 degrees before doing anything else.
2. Coat your pieces of eggplant with egg then with bread crumbs.
3. Now lay the veggies on a cookie sheet and cook them in the oven for 6 mins. Flip the eggplants and cook them for 6 more mins.
4. Coat the bottom of a casserole dish with pasta sauce then layer some of your eggplants in the dish.
5. Top the veggies with some parmesan and mozzarella then layer your eggplants, sauce, and cheese.
6. Continue this pattern until all the ingredients have been used up.
7. Finally coat the layer with some basil and cook everything in the oven for 40 mins.
8. Enjoy.

ROMAN
Fun Pasta

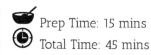

Prep Time: 15 mins
Total Time: 45 mins

Servings per Recipe: 6
Calories	656 kcal
Fat	42.1 g
Carbohydrates	50.9g
Protein	20.1 g
Cholesterol	111 mg
Sodium	1088 mg

Ingredients

1 (12 oz.) package bow tie pasta
2 tbsps olive oil
1 lb sweet Italian sausage, casings
removed and crumbled
1/2 tsp red pepper flakes
1/2 C. diced onion
3 cloves garlic, minced

1 (28 oz.) can Italian-style plum
tomatoes, drained and coarsely diced
1 1/2 C. heavy cream
1/2 tsp salt
3 tbsps minced fresh parsley

Directions

1. Boil your pasta in water and salt for 9 mins then remove the liquids.
2. Begin to stir fry your pepper flakes and sausage in oil until it the meat is browned then add the garlic and onions.
3. Let the onions cook until they are soft then add in the salt, cream, and tomatoes.
4. Stir the mix then get everything gently boiling.
5. Let the mix gently cook with a low level of heat for 9 mins then add in the pasta.
6. Stir the mix, to evenly cook the noodles, then coat everything with parsley.
7. Enjoy.

Zucchini and Spinach Soup

Prep Time: 10 mins
Total Time: 50 mins

Servings per Recipe: 6
Calories	385 kcal
Fat	24.4 g
Carbohydrates	22.5g
Protein	18.8 g
Cholesterol	58 mg
Sodium	1259 mg

Ingredients

1 lb Italian sausage
1 clove garlic, minced
2 (14 oz.) cans beef broth
1 (14.5 oz.) can Italian-style stewed tomatoes
1 C. sliced carrots
2 small zucchini, cubed
1 (14.5 oz.) can great Northern beans, undrained
2 C. spinach - packed, rinsed and torn
1/4 tsp ground black pepper
1/4 tsp salt

Directions

1. Stir fry your garlic and sausage, in a large pot, for 2 mins then combine in the pepper, broth, salt, tomato, and carrots.
2. Stir the mix, place a lid on the pot, and let everything gently boil for 20 mins with a medium to low level of heat.
3. Now add in the zucchini and beans with their sauce.
4. Place the lid back on the pot and continue cooking everything for 17 more mins.
5. Now shut the heat, stir in the spinach, and place the lid back on the pot.
6. Let the spinach wilt for 7 mins then serve the soup.
7. Enjoy.

ITALIAN
Rump Roast

Prep Time: 15 mins
Total Time: 12 hrs 15 mins

Servings per Recipe: 10
Calories	318 kcal
Fat	15.8 g
Carbohydrates	1.6g
Protein	39.4 g
Cholesterol	100 mg
Sodium	819 mg

Ingredients

3 C. water
1 tsp salt
1 tsp ground black pepper
1 tsp dried oregano
1 tsp dried basil
1 tsp onion salt
1 tsp dried parsley

1 tsp garlic powder
1 bay leaf
1 (.7 oz.) package dry Italian-style salad dressing mix
1 (5 lb) rump roast

Directions

1. Get the following boiling in a large pot: salad dressing mix, water, salt, bay leaf, black pepper, garlic, oregano, parsley, basil, and onion salt.
2. Once the mix is boiling add the roast to the crock of a slow cooker and top the mix with the simmering liquid.
3. Place the lid on the slow cooker and let everything cook for 11 hrs with low heat.
4. Now remove the meat and shred it into pieces.
5. Place the shredded meat back into the crock pot and let it cook for 20 more mins with a low level of heat.
6. Enjoy.

Classical
Risotto

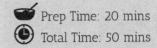 Prep Time: 20 mins

Total Time: 50 mins

Servings per Recipe: 6

Calories	431 kcal
Fat	16.6 g
Carbohydrates	56.6g
Protein	11.3 g
Cholesterol	29 mg
Sodium	1131 mg

Ingredients

6 C. chicken broth, divided
3 tbsps olive oil, divided
1 lb portobello mushrooms, thinly sliced
1 lb white mushrooms, thinly sliced
2 shallots, diced
1 1/2 C. Arborio rice
1/2 C. dry white wine

sea salt to taste
freshly ground black pepper to taste
3 tbsps finely diced chives
4 tbsps butter
1/3 C. freshly grated Parmesan cheese

Directions

1. Get your broth warm with a low level of heat. Then begin to stir fry your mushrooms in 2 tbsp of olive oil for 4 mins.

2. Now remove everything from the pot and add in 1 more tbsp of olive oil and begin to fry your shallots in it for 2 mins then add in the rice and stir fry it for 3 mins.

3. Pour in the wine while continuing to stir, and keep stirring, until it is absorbed. Once the wine has been absorbed combine in half a C. of broth and keep stirring until it is absorbed as well.

4. Now for about 20 mins keep pouring in half a C. of broth and stirring the mix until the broth is absorbed by the rice.

5. After 20 mins of forming the risotto, shut the heat and combine in: the parmesan, pepper, mushrooms and their juice, chives, salt, and butter. Enjoy.

TORTELLINI
Classico

 Prep Time: 20 mins
Total Time: 1 hr 35 mins

Servings per Recipe: 10
Calories	324 kcal
Fat	20.2 g
Carbohydrates	19.1g
Protein	14.6 g
Cholesterol	50 mg
Sodium	1145 mg

Ingredients

1 lb sweet Italian sausage, casings removed
1 C. diced onion
2 cloves garlic, minced
5 C. beef broth
1/2 C. water
1/2 C. red wine
4 large tomatoes - peeled, seeded and diced

1 C. thinly sliced carrots
1/2 tbsp packed fresh basil leaves
1/2 tsp dried oregano
1 (8 oz.) can tomato sauce
1 1/2 C. sliced zucchini
8 oz. fresh tortellini pasta
3 tbsps diced fresh parsley

Directions

1. In a large pot brown your sausage all over.
2. Then remove the meat from the pan.
3. Begin to stir fry your garlic and onions in the drippings then add in: the sausage, broth, tomato sauce, water, oregano, wine, basil, tomatoes, and carrots.
4. Get the mix boiling, set the heat to low, and let everything cook for 35 mins.
5. Remove any fat which rises to the top then add in the parsley and zucchini.
6. Continue cooking the mix for 20 more mins before adding in the pasta and letting everything cooking 15 more mins.
7. When serving the dish top it with parmesan. Enjoy.

Printed in Great Britain
by Amazon

21297506R00045